www.kindermusik.com

ISBN 1-58987-056-5

Library of Congress Cataloging-in-Publication Data
Todd, Traci N.
   Head, shoulders, knees, and toes / adapted by Traci N. Todd ; illustrated by Barry Gott.
      p. cm.
   "Sing to the tune of 'London Bridge is Falling Down'"—T.p.
   Summary: Presents a variation on the familiar action song which identifies parts of the body, with
additional lyrics and a different tune.

   ISBN 1-58987-056-5
   1. Children's songs—Texts. [1. Body, Human—Songs and music. 2. Songs.]   I. Gott, Barry, ill. II.
Title.
   PZ8.3.T5625Hea 2006
   782.42—dc22
   [E]   2006008807

Published in 2004 by Kindermusik International, Inc.

Do-Re-Me & You! is a trademark of Kindermusik International, Inc.

Printed in China
Second Printing, May 2006
First Printing, July 2004

Head, Shoulders, Knees, and Toes

(Sing to the tune of "London Bridge Is Falling Down")

adapted by Traci N. Todd

illustrated by Barry Gott

Head and shoulders, knees and toes,
Knees and toes,
Knees and toes.

Head and shoulders, knees and toes,
That's my body!

Eyes and ears and mouth and nose,
Mouth and nose,
Mouth and nose.

Eyes and ears and mouth and nose,
That's my body!

Tickle me, I'll laugh and squeal,
Laugh and squeal,
Laugh and squeal.

Tickle me, I'll laugh and squeal,
That's my body!

Bellybutton, hands and heels,
Hands and heels,
Hands and heels.

Bellybutton, hands and heels,
That's my body!

Ankles, thighs, and hands on hips,
Hands on hips,
Hands on hips.

Ankles, thighs, and hands on hips,
That's my body!

Jump and wave and blow a kiss,
Blow a kiss,
Blow a kiss.

Jump and wave and blow a kiss,
That's my body!

Elbows, wrists, and one, two feet,
One, two feet,
One, two feet.

Elbows, wrists, and one, two feet,
That's my body!

Chest and back and little seat,
Little seat,
Little seat.

Chest and back and little seat,
That's my body!

Thumbs and fingers fasten shoes,
Fasten shoes,
Fasten shoes.

Thumbs and fingers fasten shoes,
That's my body!

Hair and neck and tummy, too,
Tummy, too,
Tummy, too.

Hair and neck and tummy, too,
That's my body!

Smiling cheeks and one proud chin,
One proud chin,
One proud chin.

Smiling cheeks and one proud chin,
That's my body!

Wiggle, giggle, clap and spin,
Clap and spin,
Clap and spin.

Wiggle, giggle, clap and spin,
Now we're done!

Head, Shoulders, Knees, and Toes

traditional

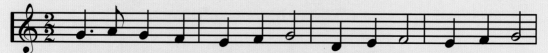

Head and shoul-ders, knees and toes, knees and toes, knees and toes.

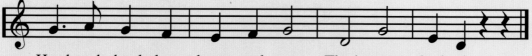

Head and shoul-ders, knees and toes. That's my bod-y!